Classic

FRENCH

Classic
FRENCH

Delicious regional recipes from France

FOREWORD BY
MARIE-PIERRE MOINE

SMITHMARK

This edition published in 1996 by
SMITHMARK Publishers, a division of US Media Holdings, Inc
16 East 32nd Street
New York NY 10016
USA

SMITHMARK books are available for bulk purchase for sales promotion and for premium use. For details write or call
the Manager of Special Sales, SMITHMARK Publishers, 16 East 32nd Street, New York, NY 10016; (212) 532–6600.

Produced by Anness Publishing Limited
1 Boundary Row
London SE1 8HP

ISBN 0-8317-5981-X
Publisher Joanna Lorenz
Senior Cookery Editor Linda Fraser
Cookery Editor Anne Hildyard
Designer Nigel Partridge
Illustrations Madeleine David
Photographers Karl Adamson, Edward Allwright, Steve Baxter,
Amanda Heywood and Michael Michaels
Recipes Carla Capalbo, Roz Denny, Christine France, Sarah Gates,
Shirley Gill, Norma MacMillan, Laura Washburn and Steven Wheeler
Food for photography Elizabeth Wolf-Cohen, Wendy Lee and Jane Stevenson
Stylists Hilary Guy, Blake Minton and Kirsty Rawlings
Jacket photography Amanda Heywood

Typeset by MC Typeset Ltd, Rochester, Kent
Printed and bound in China

Pictures on Frontispiece, 8 and 9: Zefa Pictures Ltd. Picture on Page 7: Michael Busselle

CONTENTS

FOREWORD

There is something about the home cooking of France which always conjures up the flavors, smells, and sounds of my childhood. When I started reading this cookbook, the recipes and their introductions brought back happy memories. That first encounter with pine nuts in the scented hot shrublands behind the Mediterranean coast, an early morning bicycle ride through lush Normandy pastures and a Camembert tasting at Pont-Audemer market, an autumn afternoon train journey followed by a meal that concluded with the best chocolate cream puffs I ever ate – the selection of recipes successfully evoked happy recollections of the French countryside.

When I looked at the recipes more critically, as an expatriate cook, I also appreciated the fact that despite being genuinely French, they were also accessible for kitchens anywhere in the world. Here is a collection of dishes you can very easily re-create at home with grocery store ingredients. Some recipes have been given a little twist to make them exciting for more adventurous modern tastebuds: crispy potato cakes are paired with goat cheese, curried mussels are delectably combined with lentils, sole goujons are enhanced by a sharp lime mayonnaise. Old favorites, those authentic dishes that cannot really be improved on, are presented in traditional but feasible versions. Try such dishes as Trout with Mushroom Sauce, Onion Tart, Breton Pork and Bean Casserole, or Apricot and Almond Jalousie, and discover the essence of French home cooking at its best.

MARIE-PIERRE MOINE

INTRODUCTION

rance is deservedly famous for its excellent food, and traveling through France, sampling regional dishes, is a true treat for the tastebuds.

The very size of the country means there are considerable variations in terms of climate and landscape. Ever since the time when poor communications made every region dependent on its own produce, each area has had its own specialties. Markets are a marvelous source of basic raw ingredients, which are always chosen with considerable care, be they fresh vegetables, fruit, wines, or cheeses. France is renowned for its cheeses. Every region has its own, made from cow's, goat's or ewe's milk and varying from soft and creamy to hard and strong.

The Brittany coastline is well known for its abundant seafood, particularly shellfish such as mussels, crabs, lobsters, and oysters.

Seafood, especially sole, also comes from neighboring Normandy, a region equally notable for its rich dairy pastures. Famous cheeses like Camembert, Pont-L'Evêque and Neufchâtel are produced here, along with rich butter, crème fraîche (the thick, slightly acidic cream), and fresh cream cheeses such as fromage blanc. Normandy is also famous for its apple orchards, the fruit of which is made into cider and Calvados. Bénédictine, the herb liqueur, is another Norman specialty. The meat of the region is excellent, especially pork and lamb. The popular tripe dish, *Tripes à la Mode de Caen,* is famous the world over.

Apart from the obvious, Champagne is known for charcuterie, including smoked and stuffed tongue, and game, while Lorraine lends its name to a number of dishes, including the famous quiche. Alsace numbers pork, goose, game, and choucroute (pickled cabbage) among its specialties, whereas the Burgundy

Freshly picked garlic and lemons for sale on a market stall (left), vines planted in neat rows, stretch as far as the eye can see (above), and an interesting selection of French cheeses in a typical Paris market (right).

region produces not only fine wines, but also beef and chickens, hence the recipe for Coq au Vin in this book. This is also the home of snails and Dijon mustard. From the Auvergne comes a large variety of cheeses, and also potatoes, cabbages, lentils, ham, sausages, and pork products. The cows of the mountain-

ous Savoie produce more milk than the population can drink, so this area is known for its gratin dishes using milk, cream, and cheese. Comté cheese, walnuts, chestnuts, fruit, dried beef, and wild mushrooms also come from here.

Further south is Provence, an area world-renowned for its colorful, piquant dishes. Olives and olive oil, tomatoes, onions, garlic, and herbs are ingredients that find their way into a range of recipes, including Salade Niçoise and Mediterranean Fish Stew.

The south-west is one of the great larders of France, producing lamb, Bayonne ham, beef, duck, chicken, onions, prunes, peaches, pears, grapes, and seafood, especially squid, sardines, anchovies, and oysters.

Bordeaux is known for its fine wines and Cognac, while not far away, in the Dordogne, the specialties are geese, ducks, and truffles (often used in pâtés), nuts, and fruit. In the Loire valley, both vegetables and fruits are grown, and from its river come freshwater fish such as trout. This is also the region where the legendary Tarte Tatin, with its delicious topping of caramelized apples, was first created.

From the Loire it is but a short step to Brittany, where our whistle-stop culinary tour began. As the recipes amply illustrate, France is indeed a country where one is spoilt for choice.

LEEK TERRINE WITH DELI MEATS
Terrine de Poireaux Charcutière

This attractive appetizer is very simple to make yet looks spectacular. You can make the terrine a day ahead and keep it covered in the fridge. If your guests are vegetarian offer a selection of French cheeses instead of sliced meats.

INGREDIENTS
20–24 small young leeks
4 tablespoons walnut oil
4 tablespoons olive oil
2 tablespoons white wine vinegar
1 teaspoon whole-grain mustard
about ½ pound sliced meats, such as
Jambon de Bayonne *or* Jambon de Toulouse
⅔ cup walnuts, toasted and chopped
salt and ground black pepper

SERVES 6

COOK'S TIP
For this terrine, it is important to use tender young leeks. The white part mainly is used in this recipe, but the green tops can be used in soups. The terrine must be pressed for at least 4 hours – to make it easier to slice.

1 Cut off the roots and most of the green part from the leeks. Wash thoroughly under cold running water. Bring a large pan of salted water to a boil. Add the leeks, bring the water back to a boil, then reduce the heat and simmer for 6–8 minutes, until the leeks are just tender. Drain well.

2 Fill a 1-pound loaf pan with the leeks, placing them alternately head to tail, to create a patterned effect, and sprinkling each layer with salt and pepper as you go.

3 Put another loaf pan inside the first one and gently press down on the leeks. Carefully invert both pans and let any water drain out. Place one or two kitchen weights or heavy cans on top of the pans and chill the terrine for at least 4 hours, or overnight.

4 Meanwhile, to make the dressing, spoon the walnut and olive oils, wine vinegar, and whole-grain mustard into a small bowl, add salt and pepper, and whisk together. Taste for seasoning and add more salt and pepper if required.

5 Carefully turn out the terrine on to a board and cut into slices using a large sharp knife. Lay the slices of leek terrine on serving plates and arrange the slices of meat alongside. Spoon the dressing over the slices of terrine and sprinkle over the chopped walnuts. Serve immediately.

ONION SOUP

Soupe à l'Oignon

Recipes for onion soup vary around the world, but this is the absolute classic – once the morning pick-me-up for workers at Les Halles, the food market in central Paris.

INGREDIENTS

2 tablespoons butter
1 tablespoon oil
3 large onions, thinly sliced
1 teaspoon soft brown sugar
1 tablespoons flour
2 × 10-ounce cans condensed
beef consommé
2 tablespoons medium sherry
2 teaspoons Worcestershire sauce
8 slices baguette
1 tablespoon whole-grain mustard
1 cup Gruyère cheese, shredded
salt and ground black pepper
chopped fresh parsley, to garnish

SERVES 4

1 Heat the butter and oil in a large pan and add the onions and brown sugar. Cook gently for about 20 minutes, stirring occasionally, until the onions start to turn golden brown.

2 Stir in the flour and cook for another 2 minutes. Pour in the consommé, plus two cans of water, then add the sherry and Worcestershire sauce. Season well, cover, and simmer gently for 25–30 minutes.

VARIATION
Omit the mustard and, instead, rub the croûtes on each side with the cut side of a garlic clove before adding the Gruyère cheese.

3 Preheat the broiler and, just before serving, toast the bread lightly on both sides. Spread one side of each slice with the mustard and top with the shredded cheese. Broil the toasts until bubbling and golden.

4 Ladle the soup into soup plates. Place two croûtes on top of each plate of soup and garnish with chopped fresh parsley. Serve at once.

CAMEMBERT FRITTERS

Beignets de Camembert

T hese deep-fried cheeses are simple to prepare. They are served with a red onion marmalade which can be made in advance and stored in the fridge.

INGREDIENTS
8 individual portions of Camembert
1 egg, beaten
1 cup dried bread crumbs, to coat
oil, for deep-frying
fresh parsley sprigs, to garnish

FOR THE MARMALADE
3 tablespoons sunflower oil
3 tablespoons olive oil
2 pounds red onions, sliced
1 tablespoon coriander seeds, crushed
2 bay leaves
3 tablespoons granulated sugar
6 tablespoons red wine vinegar
2 teaspoons salt

SERVES 4

1 To make the marmalade, heat the oils in a large saucepan and gently fry the onions, covered, for 20 minutes or until soft. Add the remaining ingredients, stir well, and cook, uncovered, for 10–15 minutes until most of the liquid is absorbed. Leave to cool.

2 To prepare the cheese, scratch the rinds lightly with a fork. Dip first in egg and then in bread crumbs to coat well. Dip and coat a second time if necessary. Set aside.

3 Pour oil into a deep-fat fryer to one-third full and heat to 375°F. Add the cheeses a few at a time and fry for about 2 minutes until golden. Drain on paper towels and fry the rest of the cheeses, reheating the oil in between. Serve hot with the marmalade. Garnish with parsley sprigs.

COOK'S TIP
You could make these fritters with fingers of firm Brie, or try using small rounds of goat cheese.

14

SPINACH SALAD WITH BACON AND SHRIMP

Salade d'Épinards à la Poitrine Fumée et aux Crevettes

Serve this warm salad with plenty of crusty bread for mopping up the delicious juices. It tastes every bit as good as it looks.

INGREDIENTS
7 tablespoons olive oil
2 tablespoons sherry vinegar
2 garlic cloves, finely chopped
1 teaspoon Dijon mustard
12 cooked unshelled jumbo shrimp
4 ounces lean streaky bacon, rinded and cut into strips
about 4 ounces fresh young spinach leaves
½ head oak-leaf lettuce, roughly torn
salt and ground black pepper

SERVES 4

1 To make the dressing, whisk together 6 tablespoons of the olive oil with the vinegar, garlic, mustard, and seasoning in a small pan. Heat gently until thickened slightly, then keep warm.

2 Carefully pull off the heads, then remove the shells and legs from the shrimp, leaving the tails intact. Set aside.

3 Heat the remaining oil in a frying pan and fry the bacon until golden and crisp, stirring occasionally. Add the shrimp and stir-fry for a few minutes until they are completely warmed through.

4 Meanwhile, arrange the spinach leaves and roughly torn oak-leaf lettuce leaves on four individual serving plates.

5 Spoon the bacon and shrimp on to the salad leaves, then pour over the hot dressing. Serve at once.

RED ONION GALETTES

Galettes à l'Oignon Rouge

o give these savory pastries a sharp edge, sprinkle some chopped anchovies over them before baking.

INGREDIENTS
4–5 tablespoons olive oil
1¼ pounds red onions, sliced
1 garlic clove, crushed
2 tablespoons chopped fresh mixed herbs,
such as thyme, parsley, and basil
½ pound ready-made puff pastry
1 tablespoon sun-dried tomato paste
ground black pepper
fresh thyme sprigs, to garnish

SERVES 4

1 Heat 2 tablespoons of the oil in a pan and add the onions and garlic. Cook, covered, for 15–20 minutes, stirring occasionally, until soft but not browned. Stir in the herbs.

2 Preheat the oven to 425°F. Divide the pastry into four equal pieces and roll out each one to a 6-inch round on a lightly floured surface.

3 Flute the edges by crimping them with your fingers *(left)*. Prick all over with a fork. Place the rounds on baking sheets and chill them for 10 minutes.

4 Mix 1 tablespoon of the remaining olive oil with the sun-dried tomato paste and brush over the centers of the rounds, leaving a ½-inch border. Spread the onion mixture over the pastry rounds and grind over plenty of pepper. Drizzle over a little more oil, then bake for about 15 minutes, until the pastry is crisp and golden. Serve hot, garnished with thyme sprigs.

POTATO CAKES WITH GOAT CHEESE

Petites Galettes de Pommes de Terre au Chèvre

C rispy potato cakes form the base of this melt-in-your-mouth appetizer. The goat cheese and green salad transform it from the peasant dish it was originally to *haute cuisine*.

INGREDIENTS

1 pound potatoes, coarsely grated
2 teaspoons chopped fresh thyme
1 garlic clove, crushed
2 scallions, finely chopped
2 tablespoons olive oil
4 tablespoons sweet butter
2 × 2½-ounce Crottins de Chavignol *(firm goat cheeses)*
salt and ground black pepper
fresh thyme sprigs, to garnish
mixed green salad, to serve

SERVES 2–4

1 Using your hands, squeeze out the moisture from the potatoes, then carefully combine with the chopped thyme, garlic, scallions, and seasoning.

2 Heat half of the oil and butter in a nonstick frying pan. Add two large spoonfuls of the potato mixture and press firmly down with a spoon. Cook for 3–4 minutes on each side until golden.

3 Drain the potato cakes on paper towels and keep warm. Make two more potato cakes in the same way with the remaining mixture. Meanwhile, preheat the broiler.

4 Cut the cheeses in half horizontally. Place one half cheese, cut-side up, on each potato cake *(right)*. Broil for 2–3 minutes until golden. Garnish with thyme sprigs and serve at once with the salad.

SALADE MOUCLADE
Salade Mouclade aux Lentilles

Mouclade is a traditional recipe from La Rochelle in south-western France. The dish consists of mussels in a light, creamy curry sauce and is usually served hot. Here the flavors appear in a salad of warm lentils and lightly cooked spinach. Serve at room temperature during the summer months.

INGREDIENTS
*3 tablespoons olive oil, plus extra
for drizzling
1 onion, finely chopped
1¾ cups Puy or green lentils, soaked
for 2 hours
3¾ cups vegetable broth
4–4½ pounds live mussels
5 tablespoons dry white wine
½ teaspoon mild curry paste
pinch of saffron
2 tablespoons heavy cream
2 large carrots, peeled
4 celery stalks
2 pounds young spinach, stems removed
1 tablespoon garlic oil
salt and cayenne pepper*

SERVES 4

1 Heat the oil in a heavy saucepan and soften the onion for 6–8 minutes. Add the drained lentils and vegetable broth, bring to a boil and simmer for 45 minutes. Remove from the heat and and leave to cool.

2 Scrub the mussels well under cold running water. Remove the beards and discard any mussels that are open. Place in a large saucepan and add the wine. Cover and cook over high heat, shaking the pan occasionally, for 5–8 minutes until the mussels have opened. Drain the mussels, reserving the liquid. Discard any not open. Allow to cool, then remove the shells.

3 Pass the mussel liquid through a fine strainer into a wide shallow saucepan, to remove any grit. Add the curry paste and saffron, then reduce over high heat until almost dry. Remove from the heat, stir in the cream, season, and mix with the mussels.

4 Bring a saucepan of salted water to a boil. Cut the carrot and celery into 2-inch julienne strips, cook for 3 minutes, then remove from the pan, cool, and drizzle with olive oil.

5 Wash the spinach, put the wet leaves into a large saucepan, cover, and steam for 30 seconds. Drain the spinach under cold running water, then put the leaves into a colander and press dry with the back of a large spoon. Toss the spinach with the garlic oil, season with salt and cayenne pepper, and set aside.

6 Spoon the lentils into the center of four large plates. Place five little piles of spinach around the edge of each one and put some carrot and celery strips on top of each pile. Spoon the mussels over the lentils and serve at room temperature.

GOLDEN CHEESE PUFFS

Aigrettes au Fromage

S erve these deep-fried puffs – known as *aigrettes* – with a fruity chutney and a green salad. Smaller, bite-size ones make excellent party snacks.

INGREDIENTS
½ cup flour
1 tablespoon butter
1 egg, plus 1 egg yolk, beaten
1 cup finely shredded mature
Cheddar cheese
1 tablespoon shredded Parmesan cheese
½ teaspoon mustard powder
pinch of cayenne pepper
oil, for frying
salt and ground black pepper
mango chutney and salad, to serve

SERVES 4

1 Sift the flour on to a square of wax paper and set aside. Place the butter and ⅔ cup water in a saucepan and heat until the butter is melted.

2 Bring the liquid to a boil and quickly tip in the flour all at once. Remove the pan from the heat and stir well with a wooden spoon until the mixture begins to leave the sides of the pan and forms a ball. Allow the mixture to cool slightly.

3 Gradually add the egg to the mixture, beating well after each addition. Stir in the cheeses, mustard, cayenne, and season.

4 Heat the oil in a large saucepan or deep-fat frier to 375°F or until a cube of bread browns in 30 seconds. Drop four spoonfuls of the cheese mixture at a time into the hot oil and deep-fry for 2–3 minutes until golden. Using a slotted spoon, lift out the cheese puffs and leave them to drain on paper towels. Keep them hot in the oven while cooking the remaining mixture. Allow two puffs per person, and serve immediately with a generous spoonful of mango chutney and a green salad.

GREEN BEANS WITH HAM

Haricots Verts à la Poitrine Fumée

The subtle flavors of beans and unsmoked bacon combine well in this simple peasant dish. If you like, stir in some chopped fresh parsley just before serving.

INGREDIENTS
1 pound green beans
3 tablespoons olive oil
1 onion, thinly sliced
2 garlic cloves, finely chopped
3 ounces unsmoked bacon, rinded and chopped
salt and ground black pepper

SERVES 4

1 Cook the beans in boiling salted water for about 5–6 minutes, until just tender but still with a bit of bite.

2 Meanwhile, heat the oil in a pan, add the onion and fry for 5 minutes, until softened. Remove the onion and set aside. Add the garlic and bacon *(right)* and cook for 5 minutes. Return the onions to the pan.

3 Drain the beans, add to the pan and cook, stirring occasionally, for 2–3 minutes. Season well and serve hot.

MARINATED GOAT CHEESE WITH HERBS

Fromage de Chèvre aux Herbes et à l'Huile d'Olive

These little cheeses are delicious spread on toasted slices of baguette, brushed with olive oil and rubbed with garlic.

INGREDIENTS
*4 fresh soft goat cheeses, halved
6 tablespoons chopped fresh mixed
parsley, thyme, and oregano
2 garlic cloves, chopped
12 black peppercorns, lightly crushed
⅔ cup extra virgin olive oil
salad leaves, to serve*

SERVES 4–8

COOK'S TIP
Any herbs can be added to the marinade – try chervil, tarragon, chives, and basil. If you prefer, reserve the herb-flavored oil, and use it to make a salad dressing.

1 Arrange the individual fresh goat cheeses in a single layer in a large shallow non-metallic dish.

2 Put the chopped herbs, garlic, and crushed peppercorns in a blender or food processor. Start the machine, then pour in the oil and process until the mixture is fairly smooth.

3 Spoon the herb mixture over the cheeses, then cover and leave to marinate in the fridge for 24 hours, basting the cheeses occasionally.

4 Remove the cheeses from the fridge about 30 minutes before serving and allow them to come to room temperature.

5 Serve the cheeses on a bed of salad leaves and spoon over a little of the olive oil and herb mixture.

VARIATION
For a subtle flavor and an attractive color contrast, use pink peppercorns instead of black.

SALADE NIÇOISE
Salade Niçoise

alade Niçoise is the happy marriage of tuna fish, hard-boiled eggs, green beans, and potatoes.

INGREDIENTS
1½ pounds potatoes, peeled
½ pound green beans, trimmed
3 eggs, hard-boiled
1 Romaine lettuce
½ cup French dressing, (see box below)
½ pound small plum tomatoes, quartered
14-ounce can tuna in oil, drained
1 ounce canned anchovy fillets
2 tablespoons capers
12 black olives
salt and ground black pepper
basil leaves, to garnish (optional)

SERVES 4

COOK'S TIP
To make the French dressing, put 1½ tablespoons white wine vinegar, 2 tablespoons olive oil, 1 teaspoon Dijon mustard, and 2 tablespoons chopped, fresh mixed herbs in a screw-top jar, add salt and ground black pepper to taste and shake together.

1 Bring the potatoes to a boil in salted water and cook for 20 minutes. Boil the green beans for 6 minutes. Drain the potatoes and beans under cold running water and leave to cool.

2 Slice the potatoes thickly, and shell and quarter the eggs. Wash the lettuce and dry in a salad spinner or on a clean dish towel, then chop the leaves roughly. Put the lettuce into a large salad bowl and toss with half of the dressing.

3 Put the cooled potatoes, whole green beans, and quartered tomatoes into a bowl and toss with the remaining French dressing, then arrange them decoratively over the bed of salad leaves in the salad bowl.

4 Break up the tuna fish into large flakes with a fork and distribute over the salad with the anchovy fillets, capers, and olives. Season to taste with salt and pepper and serve immediately. If you like, garnish with basil leaves.

BROILED GARLIC MUSSELS

Moules Gratinées

The crunchy crumb topping provides a good contrast to the succulent mussels underneath in this flavorsome dish.

INGREDIENTS
3–3½ pounds live mussels
½ cup dry white wine
4 tablespoons butter
2 shallots, finely chopped
2 garlic cloves, crushed
6 tablespoons dried white bread crumbs
4 tablespoons chopped fresh mixed herbs, such as Italian parsley, basil, and oregano
2 tablespoons freshly shredded Parmesan cheese
salt and ground black pepper
basil leaves, to garnish

SERVES 4

1 Scrub the mussels under cold running water. Remove the beards and discard any mussels that are open. Place in a pan with the wine. Cover and cook over high heat, shaking the pan occasionally, for 5–8 minutes until the mussels have opened.

2 Strain the mussels and reserve the cooking liquid. Discard any that remain closed. Allow to cool slightly, then remove and discard the top half of each shell, leaving the mussels on the remaining halves.

3 Melt the butter in a large frying pan and fry the shallots until softened. Add the garlic and cook for 1–2 minutes.

4 Stir in the bread crumbs and cook, stirring, until lightly browned. Remove from the heat and stir in the herbs. Moisten with a little of the reserved mussel liquid, then season to taste with salt and pepper. Preheat the broiler.

5 Spoon the bread crumb mixture over the mussels in their shells and arrange on baking sheets. Sprinkle with the shredded Parmesan cheese.

6 Cook the mussels under the hot broiler in batches for about 2 minutes, until the topping is crisp and golden. Keep the cooked mussels warm in a low oven while broiling the remainder. Garnish with basil leaves and serve immediately.

FISH STEW

Soupe de Poisson

he broth of this dish is served as an appetizer, poured over bread, and the fish as the main course.

INGREDIENTS

2 cups cooked unshelled shrimp
1 pound mixed white fish fillets
3 tablespoons olive oil
1 onion, chopped
1 leek, sliced
1 carrot, diced
1 garlic clove, chopped
½ teaspoon ground turmeric
⅔ cup dry white wine
14-ounce can chopped tomatoes
fresh parsley, thyme, and fennel sprigs
small piece of orange peel
1 cleaned squid, sliced
12 live mussels
salt and ground black pepper
Parmesan cheese shavings and chopped fresh parsley, to garnish

FOR THE ROUILLE SAUCE

2 slices white bread, crusts removed
2 garlic cloves, crushed
½ fresh red chili
1 tablespoon tomato paste
3–4 tablespoons olive oil

SERVES 4

1 Peel the shrimp leaving the tails on; cover and chill. Place all the shrimp and fish trimmings in a pan and cover with about 1⅞ cups water. Bring to a boil, then cover the pan and simmer for 30 minutes. Strain and reserve the stock.

2 Heat the oil in a large saucepan and add the onion, leek, carrot, and garlic. Fry gently for 6–7 minutes, stir in the turmeric, wine, tomatoes and juice, fish broth, herbs, and orange peel. Bring to a boil, cover, and simmer for about 20 minutes.

3 Meanwhile to make the rouille sauce, process the bread in a food processor or blender with the garlic, chili, and tomato paste. With the motor running, pour in the oil in a thin drizzle, until the mixture is smooth and thickened.

4 Add the fish and seafood to the pan and simmer for 5–6 minutes, or until the fish is opaque and the mussels open. Remove the orange peel. Season. Serve in bowls with a spoonful of the rouille sauce and sprinkled with Parmesan and parsley.

MEDITERRANEAN PLAICE ROLLS

Roulades de Carrelets

S un-dried tomatoes, pine nuts, and anchovies make a flavorsome combination for the stuffing mixture for these plaice fillets.

INGREDIENTS
4 plaice fillets, about ½ pound
each, skinned
6 tablespoons butter
1 small onion, chopped
1 celery stalk, finely chopped
2 cups fresh white bread crumbs
3 tablespoons chopped fresh parsley
2 tablespoons pine nuts, toasted
3–4 pieces sun-dried tomatoes in oil,
drained and chopped
2-ounce can anchovy fillets, drained
and chopped
5 tablespoons fish broth
ground black pepper

SERVES 4

1 Preheat the oven to 350°F. Cut the plaice fillets in half lengthwise to make eight smaller fillets.

2 Melt the butter in a pan and add the onion and celery. Cover and cook for 15 minutes, until soft. Do not brown.

3 Combine the bread crumbs, parsley, pine nuts, sun-dried tomatoes, and anchovies. Stir in the softened vegetables with the buttery juices and season with pepper.

4 Divide the stuffing into eight portions. Taking one portion at a time, form the stuffing into balls, then roll up each one inside a plaice fillet. Firmly secure each roll with a toothpick.

5 Place the rolled-up fillets in a buttered ovenproof dish. Pour in the broth and cover the dish with a piece of buttered foil. Bake for about 20 minutes, or until the fish flakes easily when tested with a fork. Remove the toothpicks, then serve the plaice rolls with a little of the cooking juices drizzled over.

SOLE GOUJONS WITH LIME MAYONNAISE

Goujons de Sole Mayonnaise au Citron Vert

This simple dish can be rustled up very quickly. It makes an excellent light lunch or supper. If you cannot find a lime, use a small lemon instead.

INGREDIENTS
⅞ cup good-quality mayonnaise
1 small garlic clove, crushed
2 teaspoons capers, rinsed and chopped
2 teaspoons chopped cornichons
finely grated rind of ½ lime
2 teaspoons lime juice
1 tablespoon chopped fresh cilantro
1½ pounds sole fillets, skinned
2 eggs, beaten
2 cups fresh white bread crumbs
oil, for deep-frying
salt and ground black pepper
lime wedges, to serve

SERVES 4

2 Cut the sole fillets into finger-length strips. Dip into the beaten egg, then into the bread crumbs.

3 Heat the oil in a deep-fat fryer to 350°F. Add the fish in batches and fry until golden brown and crisp. Drain the goujons well on paper towels.

4 Pile the goujons on to warmed serving plates and serve them with the lime wedges for squeezing over. Hand round the lime mayonnaise separately.

1 To make the lime mayonnaise, mix together the mayonnaise, garlic, capers, cornichons, lime rind and juice, and chopped cilantro. Season to taste with salt and pepper. Transfer to a serving bowl and chill until required.

RED SNAPPER WITH FENNEL

Rougets au Fenouil

Whole red snapper are excellent cooked in this way – you'll need only two fish if they are large. The lemon butter is an excellent accompaniment.

INGREDIENTS
3 small fennel bulbs
4 tablespoons olive oil
2 small onions, thinly sliced
2–4 basil leaves
4 small or 2 large red snapper, cleaned
grated rind of ½ lemon
⅔ cup fish broth
4 tablespoons butter
juice of 1 lemon

SERVES 4

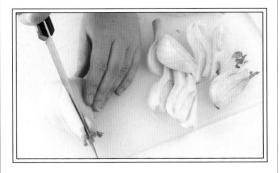

1 Snip off the feathery fronds from the fennel, chop finely and reserve for the garnish. Cut the fennel into wedges, leaving the layers attached at the root ends.

2 Heat the oil in a frying pan large enough to take the fish in a single layer. Add the fennel and onions and cook for 10–15 minutes, until softened and lightly browned.

3 Tuck a basil leaf inside each red snapper, then place the fish on top of the vegetables in the frying pan. Sprinkle the lemon rind over the fish. Pour in the broth and bring just to a boil. Cover the pan and cook gently for 15–20 minutes, until the fish are just tender.

4 Melt the butter in a small pan and, when it starts to sizzle and color slightly, add the lemon juice. Pour the sauce over the fish, sprinkle with the reserved fennel fronds and serve immediately.

TAGLIATELLE WITH SAFFRON MUSSELS
Pâtes aux Moules Safranées

Mussels in a saffron and cream sauce are served with tagliatelle in this recipe, but you can use any other pasta if you prefer.

INGREDIENTS
4–4½ pounds live mussels
⅔ cup dry white wine
2 shallots, chopped
12 ounces dried tagliatelle
2 tablespoons butter
2 garlic cloves, crushed
1 cup heavy cream
generous pinch of saffron strands
1 egg yolk
salt and ground black pepper
2 tablespoons chopped fresh parsley, to garnish

SERVES 4

1 Scrub the mussels well under cold running water. Remove the beards and discard any mussels that are open. Place in a large pan with the wine and shallots. Cover and cook over high heat, shaking the pan occasionally, for 5–8 minutes, until the mussels have opened. Drain, reserving the liquid. Discard any not open. Shell all but a few of the mussels. Keep warm.

2 Cook the tagliatelle in a large pan of boiling salted water for about 10 minutes, until *al dente*.

3 Meanwhile bring the reserved cooking liquid to a boil, then reduce by half. Strain into a cup to remove any grit. Melt the butter in another saucepan and fry the garlic for 1 minute.

4 Add the mussel liquid, cream, and saffron and heat gently until the sauce thickens slightly. Off the heat, stir in the egg yolk, shelled mussels, and seasoning.

5 Drain the tagliatelle and transfer to warmed plates. Spoon the sauce over, garnish with chopped parsley and the reserved mussels and serve at once.

CHILI SHRIMP

Grosses Crevettes à la Tomate Épicée

This spicy combination of large shrimp with tomatoes and a chopped red chili makes a lovely light main course for a casual supper. Serve with rice, noodles or freshly cooked pasta, and a leafy salad.

INGREDIENTS

3 tablespoons olive oil
2 shallots, chopped
2 garlic cloves, chopped
1 fresh red chili, chopped
1 pound ripe tomatoes, peeled, seeded,
and chopped
1 tablespoon tomato paste
1 bay leaf
1 thyme sprig
6 tablespoons dry white wine
1 pound cooked, peeled large shrimp
salt and ground black pepper
roughly torn basil leaves, to garnish

SERVES 3–4

COOK'S TIP
For a milder flavor, remove all the seeds from the chili.

1 Heat the oil in a pan, then add the shallots, garlic, and chili and fry until the garlic starts to brown.

2 Add the tomatoes, tomato paste, bay leaf, thyme, wine, and seasoning. Bring to a boil, then reduce the heat and cook gently for about 10 minutes, stirring occasionally, until the sauce has thickened. Discard the herbs.

3 Stir the shrimp into the sauce and heat through for a few minutes. Taste and adjust the seasoning. Sprinkle over the basil leaves and serve at once.

SALMON WITH WATERCRESS SAUCE

Saumon au Cresson

Adding the watercress to the sauce right at the end of cooking retains much of its flavor and color. A lovely dish for summer.

INGREDIENTS
1¼ cups heavy cream
2 tablespoons chopped fresh tarragon
2 tablespoons sweet butter
1 tablespoon sunflower oil
4 salmon fillets, about 6 ounces each, skinned and boned
1 garlic clove, crushed
½ cup dry white wine
1 bunch watercress
salt and ground black pepper
lettuce, to serve

SERVES 4

1 Gently heat the cream in a small pan until just beginning to boil. Remove from the heat and stir in half of the tarragon. Leave to infuse while cooking the fish.

2 Heat the butter and oil in a pan, add the salmon and fry for 3–5 minutes on each side. Remove and keep warm. Add the garlic and fry for 1 minute, then add the wine and boil until reduced to about 1 tablespoon.

3 Meanwhile, strip the leaves from the watercress stalks and chop finely.

4 Strain the cream into the pan and gently cook for just a few minutes, stirring until thickened. Stir in the remaining tarragon and the watercress, then cook for a few minutes, until wilted but still bright green *(right)*. Season and serve at once, spooned over the salmon. Serve with lettuce.

GRILLED SARDINES

Sardines Grillées

T he full flavor of fresh sardines needs very little to enhance it. Here it is simply complemented by lemon and parsley.

INGREDIENTS
5 tablespoons olive oil
juice of 1 lemon
1 teaspoon finely grated lemon rind
2 tablespoons chopped fresh parsley
8–12 fresh sardines (depending on size)
salt and ground black pepper
tomato and scallion salad and hot garlic bread, to serve

SERVES 4

1 Preheat the broiler. In a small bowl, mix together the oil, lemon juice and rind, parsley, and seasoning.

2 Scale the sardines under running water by rubbing the skin with your fingers from the tail towards the head. Slit the belly and remove the innards, rinse, and pat dry. Make two slashes in the skin on both sides of each sardine *(left)*.

3 Brush the sardines all over with the lemon and parsley marinade and arrange them on the broiling rack.

4 Cook under moderate heat for about 2–3 minutes, basting once, until the skin is starting to crispen, and then carefully turn the fish over. Brush with some more of the marinade. Grill for another 2–3 minutes.

5 Lift the sardines carefully on to a warmed serving platter and pour over the remaining marinade. Serve with a tomato and scallion salad and garlic bread.

TROUT WITH MUSHROOM SAUCE

Truites aux Champignons

A simple sauce made with wild or cultivated mushrooms, white wine and cream perfectly complements the flavor of trout. This recipe is a favorite all over rural France.

INGREDIENTS
8 trout fillets
seasoned flour, for dusting
6 tablespoons butter
1 garlic clove, chopped
2 teaspoons chopped fresh sage
12 ounces mixed wild or cultivated mushrooms, sliced
6 tablespoons dry white wine
1 cup heavy cream
salt and ground black pepper
fresh sage sprigs, to garnish

SERVES 4

COOK'S TIP
Use a large sharp knife to ease the skin from the trout fillets, then pull out any bones from the flesh – a pair of tweezers makes easy work of this fiddly task!

1 Remove the skin from the trout fillets, then carefully remove any bones. Lightly dust the fillets on both sides with the seasoned flour, shaking off any excess.

2 Melt the butter in a large frying pan, add the trout fillets and fry gently over moderate heat for 4–5 minutes, turning once. Remove from the pan and keep warm.

3 Add the garlic, sage, and mushrooms to the pan and fry until softened. Pour in the wine and boil briskly to allow the alcohol to evaporate. Stir in the cream and season with salt and pepper.

4 Serve the trout fillets on warmed plates with the sauce spooned over. Garnish with fresh sage sprigs.

VARIATION
Omit the sage and substitute 1 generous tablespoon pastis for the 6 tablespoons dry white wine.

COQ AU VIN

Coq au Vin

hicken joints flamed in brandy then cooked in red wine create the base of this delicious, rich casserole. Serve with potatoes and a green vegetable.

INGREDIENTS
4 tablespoons flour
3–3½ pounds chicken, cut into 8 pieces
1 tablespoon olive oil
4 tablespoons butter
20 button onions
3-ounce piece of bacon without rind, diced
about 20 button mushrooms
2 tablespoons brandy
1 bottle red Burgundy
bouquet garni
3 garlic cloves
1 teaspoon soft light brown sugar
1 tablespoon butter, softened
salt and ground black pepper
*Italian parsley, chopped fresh parsley
and croûtons, to garnish*

SERVES 4

1 Place 3 tablespoons of the flour and the seasoning in a large plastic bag and shake each chicken piece in it until lightly coated.

2 Heat the oil and butter in a large flameproof casserole. Add the onions and bacon and sauté for 3–4 minutes, until the onions are lightly browned. Add the button mushrooms and fry for 2 minutes. Remove all the vegetables with a slotted spoon, and set aside.

3 Add the chicken pieces to the hot oil and cook for about 5–6 minutes, until they are browned on all sides.

4 Pour in the brandy and (standing well back from the pan) carefully light it with a match, then shake the pan gently until the flames subside. When the flames have died down, pour in the wine, then add the bouquet garni, garlic, sugar, and seasoning.

5 Bring to a boil, cover, and simmer for 1 hour, stirring occasionally. Return the reserved onions, bacon, and mushrooms to the casserole, cover, and cook for about 30 minutes. Transfer the chicken, vegetables, and bacon to a warmed dish.

6 Remove the bouquet garni and boil rapidly for 2 minutes to reduce slightly. Cream the butter and remaining flour and whisk in teaspoonfuls of the mixture until the liquid has thickened slightly. Pour the sauce over the chicken, garnish with parsley and serve with croûtons.

POUSSINS WITH GRAPES IN VERMOUTH

Poussins aux Raisins et au Vermouth

T he aromatic herbs used to flavor vermouth, combined with sweet white grapes, make a beautiful sauce to accompany these little birds.

INGREDIENTS
4 oven-ready poussins, about
1 pound each
4 tablespoons butter, softened
2 shallots, chopped
4 tablespoons chopped fresh parsley
½ pound white grapes, preferably
muscatel, halved and seeded
⅔ cup dry white vermouth
1 teaspoon cornstarch
4 tablespoons heavy cream
salt and ground black pepper
2 tablespoons pine nuts, toasted
watercress sprigs, to garnish

SERVES 4

1 Preheat the oven to 400°F. Wash and dry the poussins. Spread the softened butter all over the birds and put a hazelnut-size piece in the cavity of each bird. Mix together the shallots and parsley.

2 Place a quarter of the shallot mixture inside each bird. Put them in a roasting pan and roast for 40–50 minutes, or until the juices run clear when the thickest part of the flesh is pierced with a skewer. Transfer to a warmed platter and keep warm.

3 Skim off most of the fat from the pan, then add the grapes and vermouth. Place the pan over low heat for a few minutes to warm the grapes.

4 Lift the grapes out of the pan with a slotted spoon and sprinkle them around the birds. Keep covered. Stir the cornstarch into the cream, then add to the pan juices. Cook gently for a few minutes, stirring, until the sauce has thickened. Taste and adjust the seasoning.

5 Pour the sauce around the poussins. Sprinkle with the toasted pine nuts and garnish with watercress sprigs.

NORMANDY PHEASANT

Faisan à la Normande

Normandy is famed for its dairy farms and apple orchards. This recipe, with its apples, cider, Calvados, butter, and cream, makes the most of its produce.

INGREDIENTS
2 oven-ready pheasants
1 tablespoon olive oil
2 tablespoons butter
4 tablespoons Calvados or Apple Jack
1⅞ cups dry cider
bouquet garni
3 eating apples, peeled, cored, and thickly sliced
⅔ cup heavy cream
salt and ground black pepper
thyme sprigs, to garnish

SERVES 4

1 Preheat the oven to 325°F. Joint both pheasants into four pieces. Discard the backbones and knuckles.

2 Heat the oil and butter in a large flameproof casserole. Working in two batches, add the pheasant pieces to the casserole and brown them over high heat. When browned, return all the pheasant pieces to the casserole.

3 Standing well back, pour the Calvados or Apple Jack over the pheasant pieces and set it alight. When the flames have subsided, pour in the cider, then add the bouquet garni and seasoning and bring to a boil. Cover and cook for 50 minutes.

4 Tuck the apple slices around the pheasant. Cover and cook for 5–10 minutes, or until the pheasant is tender. Transfer the pheasant and apple slices to a warmed serving plate, cover and keep warm. Remove the bouquet garni.

5 Reduce the sauce by half, stir in the cream and simmer for 2–3 minutes until thickened. Spoon over the pheasant and serve at once, garnished with thyme sprigs.

BRETON PORK AND BEAN CASSEROLE

Porc aux Haricots

There are many versions of this classic dish, developed in the different regions of France. Some include goose and duck as well.

INGREDIENTS

2 tablespoons olive oil
1 onion, chopped
2 garlic cloves, chopped
1 pound lean shoulder of pork, cubed
12 ounces lean lamb (preferably leg), trimmed and cubed
½ pound coarse pork and garlic sausage, cut into chunks
14-ounce can chopped tomatoes
2 tablespoons red wine
1 tablespoon tomato paste
bouquet garni
14-ounce can cannellini beans, drained
1 cup whole wheat bread crumbs
salt and ground black pepper
salad and baguette, to serve

SERVES 4

COOK'S TIP
Replace the lamb with duck breast, if you like, but be sure to drain off any fat before sprinkling with the bread crumbs.

1 Preheat the oven to 325°F. Heat the oil in a large flameproof casserole and fry the onion and garlic over low heat until softened but not browned. Remove with a slotted spoon and reserve.

2 Add the pork, lamb, and sausage cubes to the casserole, in batches if necessary, and fry over high heat for a few minutes, stirring occasionally, until they are browned on all sides. Return the onion and garlic to the casserole and stir them into the meat.

3 Stir in the tomatoes, wine, and tomato paste and add 1¼ cups water. Season well and add the bouquet garni. Cover and bring to a boil, then transfer to the oven and cook for 1½ hours.

4 Remove the bouquet garni, stir in the beans, and sprinkle the bread crumbs over the top. Return the casserole to the oven, uncovered, for 30 minutes, until the top is golden brown. Serve hot with a green salad and baguette to mop up the sauce.

RICH BEEF CASSEROLE

Boeuf au Vin Rouge

T his full-bodied dish should be served with mashed potatoes to absorb its delicious sauce. It is a perfect meal for a winter's day.

INGREDIENTS

2 pounds chuck steak, cut into cubes
2 onions, coarsely chopped
1 bouquet garni
6 black peppercorns
1 tablespoon red wine vinegar
1 bottle full-bodied red wine
4 tablespoons olive oil
3 celery stalks, thickly sliced
½ cup flour
1¼ cups beef broth
2 tablespoons tomato paste
2 garlic cloves, crushed
6 ounces brown mushrooms, halved
14-ounce can artichoke hearts, drained
and halved
chopped fresh parsley and
thyme, to garnish
creamy mashed potatoes, to serve

SERVES 4–6

1 Place the meat cubes in a large bowl. Add the onions, bouquet garni, peppercorns, vinegar, and red wine. Stir well, cover and leave to marinate overnight.

2 The next day, preheat the oven to 325°F. Using a slotted spoon, remove the meat cubes and onions from the marinade, reserving the marinade. Pat the meat and onions dry.

3 Heat the oil in a large flameproof casserole and fry the meat and onions in batches, adding a little more oil, if necessary. Remove and set aside.

4 Add the celery to the casserole and fry until lightly browned. Remove and set aside with the meat and onions.

5 Sprinkle the flour into the casserole and cook for 1 minute. Gradually add the reserved marinade and the broth, and bring to a boil, stirring. Return the meat, onions, and celery to the casserole, then stir in the tomato paste and crushed garlic.

6 Cover the casserole and cook in the oven for about 2¼ hours. Stir in the brown mushrooms and artichokes, cover again and return to the oven for another 15 minutes, until the meat is tender. Garnish with chopped parsley and thyme, and serve hot with creamy mashed potatoes.

POT-ROAST POUSSINS

Poussins au Céleri

T his method of cooking keeps the poussins moist and succulent, and provides a whole meal cooked in one dish. Serve it in spring or early summer.

INGREDIENTS
1 tablespoon olive oil
1 onion, sliced
1 large garlic clove, sliced
½ cup diced lightly smoked bacon
2 fresh poussins, just under 1 pound each
2 tablespoons butter, melted
2 baby celery hearts, each cut into 4
8 baby carrots
2 small zucchini, cut into chunks
8 small new potatoes
2½ cups chicken broth
⅔ cup dry white wine
1 bay leaf
2 fresh thyme sprigs
2 fresh rosemary sprigs
1 tablespoon butter, softened
1 tablespoon flour
salt and ground black pepper
fresh herbs, to garnish

SERVES 2-4

1 Preheat the oven to 375°F. Heat the olive oil in a large flameproof casserole, add the onion, garlic, and bacon and sauté for 5–6 minutes.

2 Brush the poussins with a little of the melted butter and season well. Lay them on top of the onion mixture and arrange the prepared vegetables around them. Pour the chicken broth and wine around the birds and add the herbs. Cover, bake for 20 minutes, then remove the lid and brush the birds with the remaining melted butter. Bake for another 25–30 minutes until golden.

3 Transfer the poussins to warmed serving plates. Remove the vegetables with a slotted spoon and arrange them round the birds. Cover with foil and keep warm.

4 Discard the herbs from the pan juices. In a bowl, mix together the butter and flour to form a thick paste. Bring the liquid in the pan to a boil and then whisk in a few teaspoonfuls of the paste, until thickened. Taste the sauce for seasoning and add salt and pepper if necessary. Serve the poussins, cut in half if wished, with the vegetables. Garnish with fresh herb sprigs.

RATATOUILLE

Ratatouille

A wonderful casserole of vegetables that can be served as an appetizer, main course or side-dish, and is equally good both hot or cold.

INGREDIENTS
2 large eggplants, coarsely chopped
4 zucchini, coarsely chopped
⅔ cup olive oil
2 onions, sliced
2 garlic cloves, chopped
1 large red bell pepper, seeded and coarsely chopped
2 large yellow bell peppers, seeded and coarsely chopped
fresh rosemary sprig
fresh thyme sprig
1 teaspoon coriander seeds, crushed
3 plum tomatoes, skinned, seeded, and chopped
8 basil leaves, torn
salt and ground black pepper
fresh parsley or basil sprigs, to garnish

SERVES 4

1 Sprinkle the eggplants and zucchini with salt, and then place them in a colander with a plate and a weight on top to extract the bitter juices. Leave them to stand for about 30 minutes.

2 Heat the olive oil in a large flameproof casserole. Add the onions, fry gently for about 6–7 minutes, until just softened, then add the garlic and cook for 2 minutes.

COOK'S TIP
For extra flavor, stir in a handful of pitted halved black or green olives immediately before serving.

3 Rinse the eggplants and zucchini and pat dry with paper towels. Add to the pan with the bell peppers, increase the heat and sauté until the bell peppers are just turning brown. Add the herbs and coriander seeds, then cover the casserole and cook gently for about 40 minutes.

4 Add the tomatoes and season well. Cook gently for 10 minutes, until the vegetables are soft but not too mushy. Remove the herb sprigs. Stir in the basil leaves and taste for seasoning. Serve warm or cold, garnished with sprigs of parsley or basil.

ONION TART

Tarte à l'Oignon

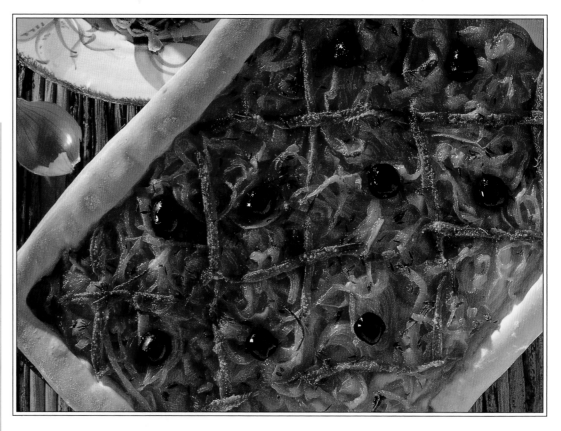

The Provençal version of pizza, this is a versatile dish that can be served hot or cold. It is ideal for summer picnics.

INGREDIENTS
10-ounce package pizza base mix
1 teaspoon olive oil, plus extra
for drizzling

FOR THE TOPPING
2 tablespoons olive oil
6 onions, thinly sliced
2 garlic cloves, crushed
2-ounce can anchovy fillets, sliced in
half lengthwise
8 black olives, pitted
2 teaspoons chopped fresh thyme, or
½ teaspoon dried thyme
salt and ground black pepper

SERVES 6

1 Make the topping, heat the oil in a frying pan, add the sliced onions and garlic and season lightly. Fry gently, stirring occasionally, for about 40 minutes, or until the onions are soft but not too brown.

2 Preheat the oven to 425°F. Empty the pizza base mix into a large bowl, stir in 1 cup warm water and add the olive oil. Mix to a dough and then turn out, and knead for about 5 minutes.

3 Lightly grease a 13 × 9-inch jelly roll pan. Roll out the dough on a lightly floured surface to fit the pan and press into the base. Spread the cooked onions evenly over the dough and then arrange the anchovy fillets on top in a lattice pattern. Sprinkle over the olives and chopped thyme and drizzle with a little olive oil. Place in a large sealed plastic bag and leave to rise in a warm place for 15 minutes.

4 Bake for 10 minutes. Reduce the oven temperature to 375°F and cook for 15–20 minutes or until the tart is golden brown around the edges. Serve warm or cold.

PROVENÇAL BEANS

Haricots à la Provençale

Much of the cuisine of Provence is based on the tomato. Here tomatoes and garlic transform plain beans into a memorable dish.

INGREDIENTS
1 teaspoon olive oil
1 small onion, finely chopped
1 garlic clove, crushed
½ pound runner beans,
trimmed and sliced
½ pound green beans,
trimmed and sliced
2 tomatoes, peeled and chopped
salt and ground black pepper

SERVES 4

1 Heat the oil in a heavy-based saucepan and sauté the onion over medium heat until softened but not browned.

2 Add the garlic and sauté for 1–2 minutes, then stir in the sliced runner beans, green beans and chopped tomatoes. Season generously with salt and pepper *(left)*, then cover the pan tightly with a lid.

3 Cook over fairly low heat, shaking the pan occasionally, for about 30 minutes, or until the beans are tender. Serve hot.

MUSHROOM MEDLEY

Fricassée de Champignons

The wonderful range of mushrooms – both fresh and dried – available in France is put to good use in this exciting side-dish.

INGREDIENTS

½-ounce package dried cèpes or porcini
mushrooms (optional)
4 tablespoons olive oil
½ pound button mushrooms,
halved or sliced
4 ounces oyster mushrooms
4 ounces fresh shiitake mushrooms, or
1 ounce dried and soaked mushrooms
2 garlic cloves, crushed
2 teaspoons ground coriander
3 tablespoons chopped fresh parsley
salt and ground black pepper

SERVES 4

2 In a large saucepan, heat the oil and add all the mushrooms, including the soaked cèpes or porcini, if using. Stir well, cover and cook gently for 5 minutes.

1 If you are using dried cèpes or porcini mushrooms (and they do give a good rich flavor), soak them in a little hot water just to cover for 20 minutes.

3 Crush the garlic and add to the pan with the coriander and seasoning. Stir well then cook for 5 minutes more, until the mushrooms are tender and much of the liquid has been reduced. Stir in the chopped parsley, then allow the mushrooms to cool slightly before serving.

POTATO GRATIN
Gratin de Pommes de Terre

This tasty potato dish is perfect for a light supper or lunch dish. For a more substantial meal, serve with roast chicken or lamb chops and add a green vegetable or salad.

INGREDIENTS
1 garlic clove
5 large baking potatoes, peeled
3 tablespoons freshly shredded
Parmesan cheese
2½ cups vegetable or chicken broth
pinch of freshly grated nutmeg
salt and ground black pepper

SERVES 4

3 Continue layering the potatoes and cheese as before, then pour over the rest of the broth. Sprinkle with nutmeg.

4 Bake in the oven for 1¼–1½ hours or until the potatoes are tender and the tops well browned.

1 Preheat the oven to 400°F. Halve the garlic clove and rub over the base and sides of a gratin dish measuring about 8 × 12 inches.

2 Slice the potatoes very thinly and arrange a third of them in the dish. Sprinkle with a little shredded cheese, salt and pepper. Pour over some of the broth.

COOK'S TIP
For a potato and onion gratin, slice an onion and layer it with the potato.

BELGIAN ENDIVE, CARROT, AND ARUGULA SALAD

Salade Mélangée d'Endives, Carottes et Roquette

A bright and colorful salad which is ideal for a buffet or barbecue party. If you cannot find arugula, if you like watercress can be used instead.

INGREDIENTS
3 carrots, coarsely shredded
about 2 ounces fresh arugula,
roughly chopped
1 large Belgian endive, separated
into leaves

FOR THE DRESSING
3 tablespoons sunflower oil
1 tablespoon hazelnut or walnut
oil (optional)
2 tablespoons cider or white wine vinegar
2 teaspoons clear honey
1 teaspoon grated lemon rind
1 tablespoon poppy seeds
salt and ground black pepper

SERVES 4–6

1 Mix together the carrots and arugula in a large bowl and season well.

2 Shake the dressing ingredients together in a screw-top jar then pour on to the carrot mixture. Toss the salad thoroughly.

3 Line shallow salad bowls with the Belgian endive and spoon the salad into the center *(right)*. Serve lightly chilled.

CHOCOLATE CHESTNUT ROULADE

Roulade au Chocolat et aux Marrons

T his moist chocolate sponge has a soft, mousse-like texture as it contains no flour. Don't worry if it cracks as you roll it up – this is typical of a good roulade.

INGREDIENTS
6 ounces semisweet chocolate
2 tablespoons strong black coffee
5 eggs, separated
¾ cup superfine sugar
1 cup heavy cream
½ pound unsweetened chestnut purée
3–4 tablespoons confectioner's sugar, plus extra for dusting
light cream, to serve

SERVES 8

1 Preheat the oven to 350°F. Line a 13 × 9-inch jelly roll pan with wax paper and brush lightly with oil.

2 Break the chocolate into a bowl and set over a saucepan of barely simmering water. Allow the chocolate to melt, then stir until smooth. Remove the bowl from the saucepan and stir in the black coffee. Leave to cool slightly.

3 Whisk together the egg yolks and superfine sugar in a separate bowl, until they are thick and light, then stir in the cooled chocolate mixture.

4 Whisk the egg whites in another bowl until they hold stiff peaks. Stir a spoonful into the chocolate mixture to lighten it, then gently fold in the rest.

5 Pour the mixture into the prepared pan, and gently spread with a rubber spatula to level the surface. Bake for 20 minutes. Remove the roulade from the oven, then cover with a clean dish towel and leave to cool in the pan for several hours, or overnight.

6 Put the heavy cream into a large bowl and whip until it forms soft peaks. In another bowl, mix together the chestnut purée and confectioner's sugar until smooth, then fold into the whipped cream.

7 Lay a piece of wax paper on the work surface and dust with confectioner's sugar. Turn out the roulade on to the paper and carefully peel off the lining paper. Trim the sides. Gently spread the chestnut cream evenly over the chocolate sponge to within 1 inch of the edges.

8 Using the wax paper to help you, carefully roll up the roulade as tightly and evenly as possible.

9 Chill the roulade for 2 hours, then sprinkle liberally with confectioner's sugar. Serve in thick slices with light cream.

COOK'S TIP
Make sure that you whisk the egg yolks and sugar for at least 5 minutes to incorporate as much air as possible.

CHOCOLATE CREAM PUFFS

Profiteroles au Chocolat

These luscious pastries are a favorite dessert in France. For perfect cream-puff pastry, it is important that the flour is added quickly and all at once to the boiling liquid.

INGREDIENTS

⅔ cup flour
pinch of salt
4 tablespoons butter
2 eggs, beaten
1⅞ cups whipping cream
4 ounces semisweet chocolate

MAKES 24

1 Preheat the oven to 425°F. Grease two baking sheets. Sift the flour and salt on to a sheet of paper. Put the butter and ⅔ cup water into a pan and heat gently until the butter has melted. Bring to a boil and then tip in the flour all at once. Remove from the heat. Beat until the mixture forms a ball and leaves the sides of the pan. Allow to cool slightly.

2 Gradually add the beaten eggs, beating well after each addition, until a smooth, thick paste is formed. Spoon into a large pastry bag with a ½-inch plain nozzle.

3 Pipe 24 walnut-size balls on to the baking sheets. Bake at the top of the oven for 20–25 minutes. Make a slit in each one for the steam to escape, then return to the oven for 5 minutes. Cool on a wire rack.

4 Place all but 4 tablespoons of the cream in a bowl, whip until just thick, then spoon into a large pastry bag fitted with a plain nozzle. Cut each cream puff in half, fill with cream and reassemble.

5 To make the chocolate sauce, place the chocolate in a pan with 4 tablespoons water and the reserved 4 tablespoons cream. Heat gently over very low heat until the chocolate has melted. Pile all the cream puffs in a pyramid on a large serving dish and pour the hot chocolate sauce over them just before serving.

TARTE TATIN
Tarte Tatin

This delicious caramelized fruit tart was created by the Tatin sisters who ran a restaurant in Sologne in the Orléanais around the turn of the century.

INGREDIENTS
FOR THE PASTRY
4 tablespoons butter, softened
3 tablespoons superfine sugar
1 egg
1 cup flour
pinch of salt

FOR THE APPLE LAYER
6 tablespoons butter, softened
generous ½ cup brown sugar
10 firm eating apples, peeled, cored and thickly sliced
whipped cream, to serve

SERVES 4

1 To make the pastry, cream the butter and sugar in a bowl until pale and creamy. Beat in the egg, then sift in the flour and salt and mix to a soft dough. Knead the dough lightly on a floured surface, then wrap in plastic wrap and chill for 1 hour.

2 Grease a 9-inch cake pan, then add 4 tablespoons of the butter. Place the cake pan on the burner and melt the butter gently. Remove and sprinkle with ⅓ cup of the brown sugar.

3 Arrange the apple slices on top, then sprinkle with the remaining sugar and dot with the remaining butter.

4 Preheat the oven to 450°F. Place the cake pan on the burner again, over low to medium heat, for about 15 minutes, until a light golden caramel forms on the bottom. Remove from the heat.

5 Roll out the pastry on a lightly floured surface to around the same size as the pan and lay on top of the apples. Tuck the pastry edges round the sides of the apples.

6 Bake the tart for about 20–25 minutes, until the pastry is golden. Remove the tart from the oven and leave it to stand for about 5 minutes.

7 Place an upturned plate on top of the cake pan and, holding the two together with a dish towel, turn the apple tart out on to the plate. Serve the tart while still warm with whipped cream.

CREPES SUZETTE

Crêpes Suzette

A n impressive dessert, ideal for serving at the end of a formal dinner party. For a special touch, flame the brandy as you pour it into the pan.

INGREDIENTS
1 cup flour
pinch of salt
1 egg
1 egg yolk
1¼ cups skim milk
1 tablespoon sweet butter, melted, plus extra for frying

FOR THE SAUCE
2 large oranges
4 tablespoons butter
generous ½ cup brown sugar
1 tablespoon Grand Marnier
1 tablespoon brandy

MAKES 8

1 Sift the flour and salt into a bowl and make a well in the center. Add the egg and the extra yolk into the well. Stir with a wooden spoon to incorporate the flour from around the edges.

2 When the mixture thickens, gradually pour on the milk, beating well after each addition, until a smooth batter is formed. Stir in the butter, transfer to a measuring cup, cover and chill.

3 Heat an 8-inch shallow frying pan, add a little butter and heat until sizzling. Pour in a little of the batter, tilting the pan back and forth to cover the base thinly.

4 Cook the crêpes over medium heat for 1–2 minutes until lightly browned underneath, then flip over with a spatula and cook for 1 minute more. Repeat this process until you have eight crêpes. Pile them up on a plate as they are ready.

5 Pare the rind from one of the oranges and reserve 1 teaspoon for decoration. Squeeze the juice from both oranges.

6 To make the sauce, melt the butter in a large frying pan and add the sugar, orange rind, and juice. Heat gently until the sugar has dissolved and the mixture is bubbling. Fold each crêpe in quarters. Add to the pan one at a time, coat in the sauce and fold in half again. Push to the side of the pan to make room for the others.

7 Pour on the Grand Marnier and brandy and cook gently for 2–3 minutes, until the sauce has slightly caramelized. Serve, sprinkled with the reserved orange rind.

PEAR AND HAZELNUT FLAN

Tarte aux Poires

A delicious flan for a special meal. If you prefer use ground almonds instead of the hazelnuts. If the filling is too thick, stir in some pear juice.

INGREDIENTS
FOR THE PASTRY
1 cup all-purpose flour
¾ cup whole-wheat flour
8 tablespoons sunflower margarine
3 tablespoons cold water

FOR THE FILLING
½ cup self-rising flour
1 cup ground hazelnuts
1 teaspoon vanilla extract
2 ounces superfine sugar
4 tablespoons butter, softened
2 eggs, beaten
3 tablespoons raspberry jam
14-ounce can pears in natural juice
chopped hazelnuts, to decorate

SERVES 6–8

1 For the pastry, stir the flours together in a mixing bowl, then rub in the margarine until the mixture resembles fine crumbs. Mix to a firm dough with the water.

2 Roll out the pastry and use it to line a 9–10-inch quiche pan, pressing it firmly up the sides after trimming, so the pastry sits above the tin a little. Prick the base, line with wax paper and fill with dried beans. Chill for 30 minutes.

3 Preheat the oven to 400°F. Place the quiche pan on a baking sheet and bake for 20 minutes, removing the paper and beans for the last 5 minutes.

4 Meanwhile to make the filling, beat together all the ingredients except for the jam and pears.

5 Reduce the oven temperature to 350°F. Spread the jam evenly on the pastry shell and spoon the filling over the jam. Drain the pears well and arrange them, cut-side down, in the filling. Sprinkle with the chopped nuts and bake for about 30 minutes until golden brown and set.

APRICOT AND ALMOND JALOUSIE

Jalousie aux Amandes et à l'Abricot

Jalousie means "shutter" in French, and the traditional slatted puff pastry topping of this fruit pie looks exactly like the shutters outside the windows of French houses.

INGREDIENTS
½ pound ready-made puff pastry
a little beaten egg
6 tablespoons apricot preserve
2 tablespoons superfine sugar
2 tablespoons sliced almonds
cream or natural yogurt, to serve

SERVES 4

1 Preheat the oven to 425°F. Roll out the pastry on a lightly floured surface and cut into a 12-inch square. Cut in half to make two rectangles.

2 Place one piece of pastry on a wetted baking sheet and brush all round the edges with beaten egg. Spread over the apricot preserve.

3 Fold the remaining rectangle in half lengthwise and cut about eight diagonal slits from the center fold to within about ½ inch of the edge all the way along.

4 Unfold the pastry and place it on top of the preserve-covered pastry on the baking sheet, matching each edge carefully to the base. Press the pastry edges together well to seal and scallop the edges at close intervals with the back of a small knife.

5 Brush the slashed pastry top with a little water and sprinkle evenly with the sugar and the sliced almonds.

6 Bake in the oven for 25–30 minutes, until well risen and golden brown. Remove the jalousie from the oven and leave to cool on a wire rack. Serve the jalousie sliced, with cream or natural yogurt.

CREME CARAMEL
Crème Caramel

T his creamy, caramel-flavored custard now enjoys worldwide popularity. Do not put too much water into the roasting pan or it may bubble over into the ramekins.

INGREDIENTS
½ cup granulated sugar
1¼ cups milk
1¼ cups light cream
6 eggs
6 tablespoons superfine sugar
½ teaspoon vanilla extract

SERVES 6

1 Preheat the oven to 300°F and half fill a large, deep roasting pan with water. Set aside until needed.

2 To make the caramel topping, place the granulated sugar in a small saucepan with 4 tablespoons water and heat it gently, swirling the pan from time to time, until the sugar is dissolved. Increase the heat and boil, without stirring, to a good caramel color.

3 Immediately pour the caramel into six ramekin dishes. Place the dishes in the roasting pan and set aside.

4 To make the egg custard, heat the milk and cream together in a pan until almost boiling. Meanwhile, beat together the eggs, superfine sugar, and vanilla extract.

5 Whisk the hot milk into the eggs and sugar, then pour the liquid through a strainer on to the cooled caramel bases.

6 Bake in the preheated oven for 1½–2 hours (topping up the water level after 1 hour), or until the custards have set in the center. Lift out the dishes and leave to cool, then cover and chill overnight.

7 Loosen the sides of the chilled custards with a knife and invert on to serving plates, allowing the caramel sauce to run down the sides.